Clandestine Black Ops: The secret criminal underworld of corporate war craft

R P CRONAN

Copyright © 2020 R P Cronan

All rights reserved.

ISBN: 9798555824127

FOREWORD

A number of years ago, our organization was targeted in very overt ways. While we were able to defend against some of these methods, we struggled with others. R P Cronan was recommended to us through a mutual contact and helped us understand what was happening to us and how to defend against it. Additionally, he helped us identify a number of covert operations our competitors were using that we had no idea about. With his help we were able to defend our enterprise, protect our employees, investors and customers and, take the fight to our rivals.

When R P Cronan told me the idea for this book, I thought it was brilliant. He is the best person to write it, having had direct experience in the shady underworld of corporate war craft, which I mean in complementary way.

I was so excited to read the first draft and even though I'd worked with him for a number of years, I was still surprised by what I read and just couldn't put the book down. The way it is structured is amazing and perfect for use as reference material to develop your own defensive strategies.

Whether you're an undergraduate, just starting your business career, leading your own enterprise or launching your own business, this book will teach you things no University degree will touch.

Yours faithfully,

Client X

CONTENTS

Foreword	i
Disclaimer	ii
Introduction	1
Attack Targets	3
Capital/Investors	4
Communications	5
Growth/New Business	6
Infrastructure	7
Insurance	8
Law	9
People	9
Revenue/Cash Flow	10
Supply Chains	11
Attack Methods	13
Arson	13
Corporate Espionage	14
Corporate Sabotage	16
Crime Agency Tip Offs	17
Criminal Damage	18
Cyber-Crime	19

Employee Poaching	21
Entrapment	21
Falsifying Information	22
Kidnap	24
Legal Action	25
Murder	27
Poison	29
Private Investigators	30
Tampering	31
Theft	32
Violence	33

DISCLAIMER

The operations, methods and techniques contained within this book are predominantly illegal and you should not use them to attack other organizations or individuals. This book is intended for educational purposes, supporting you in formulating your own defensive strategies to counter the actions of hostile rivals. Before executing any strategy, be that defensive or offensive, you must seek legal counsel. The author and publisher of this book take no responsibility for your actions or those of anyone associated with you or your organization.

INTRODUCTION

If you have purchased this book expecting to read a novel, you are out of luck. If you think this is a work of fiction, or these things only happen in large corporations, the case examples will prove just how naive you truly are.

This book is intended as a reference tool for business leaders to develop defensive strategies to protect their enterprises and, in doing so, protect the livelihoods of employees and national economic interests.

As it has been explained in the disclaimer, a lot of the material in this book is illegal and you should take legal advice before applying any of the operations, methods and techniques discussed.

Waging a war on your business rivals is acceptable, its healthy competition, but only using legal strategies and tactics. There are many hostile rivals out there that want to see your organization collapse and will wage war using the illegal actions I cover later. This book is intended to help you understand the many ways in which this could happen, so you can protect your enterprise.

Any organization that uses the operations, methods and techniques in this book to attack a rival is not only performing illegal actions that will result in custodial sentencing, but is putting their own national economic interests at risk. This may result in short term gains for their business, but can lead to long term devastation of the wider market or industry.

This book has been structured to help you identify what your rivals may attack and how they may attack it. You can read the 'Attack Targets' section, then cross reference it to relevant information in the 'Attack Methods' section.

I hope you enjoy my book and good luck with developing your strategies and tactics.

ATTACK TARGETS

While the disclaimer of this book explains how many of the techniques explored in this publication are illegal, some are not. Right now, your rivals are targeting at least one of the following areas of your business, and no doubt you are attacking them in a similar way, without breaking any laws!

For example, you may be undercutting your rival's price. This is a direct attack on their ability to generate new business and growth, which also hits their revenue streams and short term cash flow. Capitalism actively promotes such attacks, which are protected by law.

However, your business is exposed to a wide range of attacks, both legal and illegal. To understand these vulnerable areas, we must consider them individually, and how an attack can be launched. You may have other areas unique to your organization and you should consider what they are and how they can be attacked.

Remember, while I strongly recommend against it, if you choose to use any of these techniques to attack a rival business you take full responsibility for your actions and carry them out at your own risk.

Capital/Investors

Overview

To drive growth, or cover short to medium term cash flow problems, you may look to raise investment or debt capital. Damaging your ability to do so will either slow down your growth or, if you are already financially weakened, disrupt your cash flow to the point of bankruptcy.

To cause these effects, your rival will need to make you look like a significant investment risk. Of course, this is not easy to achieve because investments are based on data and the calculation of risk. However, they are also based on gut instinct and perception, which is where your rival will focus their efforts to cause maximum damage. If people believe their money is not safe in your hands, whether as an investment or loan, they will not provide those funds. The knock-on effect is to starve your organization of much needed capital or force you to seek riskier sources of funding with higher interest rates and additional strings attached. In doing so, you will be weakened and easier to attack in the future.

Equally, your rival may use violence and murder as a means of eliminating or intimidating potential investors and bankers who could provide you with funds.

As with many techniques covered in this book, your rival's success is largely dependent on focused targeting. Sustaining their attack will serve to cement negative perceptions in people's minds. It is also important to note, while other techniques may target specific geographic regions, this is an attack on your entire organization and its reputation.

Attack Targets

- Brand Credibility and Honesty
- Investor Confidence
- Safety of Operations
- Safety of Products

Attack Methods

- Corporate Espionage
- Falsifying Information
- Murder
- Private Investigators

- Violence

Communications

Overview

Communications are key for your business to service your existing customers and win new ones. Taking down your communications will disrupt your ability to engage your markets, causing you to lose customers and potential new deals. For example, your rival may stop you submitting bids or sourcing new sales leads or stop you from securing contract renewals or appeasing customers who want to leave.

While this causes significant damage, it cannot be sustained long enough to force your business into administration. However, it can cause long term damage in areas such as brand reputation, customer relationships, insurance premiums, security costs and more. In the short term you may be stopped from winning new business, causing damage to your sales pipeline growth and the loss of key customer accounts.

As with all attack techniques, sustained action against your organization will inflict the greatest losses, especially when focused on specific target market or regions.

Attack Targets

- Apps
- Direct Mail
- Email Service Providers
- Phone Systems
- Public Speakers
- Social Media
- Websites

Attack Methods

- Arson
- Corporate Espionage
- Criminal Damage
- Cyber Crime
- Falsifying Information
- Kidnap

- Poison
- Violence

Growth/New Business

Overview

Ambitious growth objectives can only be achieved by winning new business. Damaging your organization's ability to win new business will cause significant harm. For example, a downturn in commercial performance will reduce your value and hinder your ability to attract investors and/or raise capital.

Combined with a focused and sustained attack on your existing customer base, your rival can rapidly reduce you to bankruptcy. The simplest way to stop you winning new business is to completely discredit you in the markets (or a targeted market) in which you operate.

Depending on whether they attack your entire enterprise or a targeted business unit, their success can force you to retreat from a given market or region, or completely collapse.

As with attacking revenue/cash flow, a sustained campaign against your business will cause the greatest damage. If you are a larger enterprise, with multi-national or global operations, you are most likely to be attacked market-by-market or region-by-region so your rival can manage their investment in your downfall more easily.

Attack Targets

- Brand Credibility and Honesty
- Buyers of Products and/or Services
- Safety of Operations
- Safety of Products

Attack Methods

- Corporate Espionage
- Crime Agency Tips Offs
- Falsifying Information
- Murder
- Private Investigators

- Violence

Infrastructure

Overview

Increasing reliance on technical, physical and other types of infrastructure makes your organization extremely vulnerable to attack. A successful attack can have implications ranging from an increase in expenditure to outright collapse of your enterprise.

Technical infrastructure, such as IT systems and software applications, are attacked daily across the globe. This is the new normal. However, attacks on physical infrastructure are also possible and can stop business operations dead.

Attacks can be small, targeted and sustained or large one-offs. Your rival's objective is to stop your business producing added value through its ongoing operations, such as manufacturing, service delivery, logistics, customer service, communications and so on.

Attack Targets

- Buildings
- CRMs
- Electric Supplies
- Employees
- IT Systems and Equipment
- Phone and Internet Supplies
- Plant and Machinery
- Sanitation Systems
- Vehicles
- Water Supplies

Attack Methods

- Arson
- Corporate Espionage
- Corporate Sabotage
- Criminal Damage
- Cyber Crime
- Poison

- Theft

Insurance

Overview

Businesses are dependent on insurances to continue trading. Professional indemnity, employer liability and public liability are just a few critical areas where, without the right insurance cover, your organization cannot safely or legally trade.

By hitting your organization's ability to get insurance, or pushing up your premiums to prohibitive levels, you can be temporarily or permanently knocked out of the market. To do this your rival will need to challenge your insurances with substantiated and spurious claims. The former will push up your premiums and, with success in court, damage your ability to renew your insurance. The latter will enable rumor to spread throughout the media and damage your brand reputation, creating adverse effects on your insurances and other areas of your business.

Attack Targets

- Brand Credibility and Honesty
- Employees
- Insurance Protection
- Public
- Safety of Operations
- Safety of Products

Attack Methods

- Corporate Espionage
- Falsifying Information
- Legal Action
- Murder
- Private Investigators
- Violence

Law

Overview

Your rival can attack you with litigation and this tactic is as old as law itself. However, there are other ways they can use the law to attack you and the impact on your business can range from criminal investigations to reputational damage to increased legal costs.

For example, providing false or substantiated tip offs of criminal activity to the police can cause very lengthy and public investigations, which provide opportunities to capitalize on the negative publicity. Your rival can even covertly encourage and fund legal action against you on behalf of customers and/or employees. Their approach will depend on what outcome they are trying to achieve.

Attack Targets

- Corporation
- Employees
- Public

Attack Methods

- Corporate Espionage
- Crime Agency Tip Offs
- Falsifying Information
- Legal Action
- Private Investigators

People

Overview

People are your organization's greatest asset, but they are also your greatest vulnerability if your rivals know how to exploit them – and they will. Hiring private investigators to research members of your leadership team and your employees can give your rivals the keys to unlock your commercial secrets. They may even entrap members of your leadership team, or other employees, then use the evidence they have on them to their advantage.

Having damning intelligence on individuals makes them easier to manipulate. By leveraging their intelligence, they can get them to provide pricing information, trade secrets, customer lists and more. They can even get them to bug offices, perform acts of sabotage or retain them as corporate spies.

While highly unethical, this technique is probably the most effective and efficient way in which you will be attacked and means your rival won't have to do the dirty work themselves.

However, it doesn't stop there. Some rivals may hire specialists to undertake corporate sabotage in order to remove you from your own company and replace you with an individual who provides favorable treatment to your rival. This could be in the form of deals you would never sanction or to form competitive alliances, such as a cartel.

Attack Targets

- Employees

Attack Methods

- Corporate Sabotage
- Entrapment
- Murder
- Private Investigators
- Violence

Revenue/Cash Flow

Overview

Revenue is the lifeblood of any organization. Attacking your business's ability to generate revenue and/or maintain cash flow, especially for a sustained period, can cause it to collapse into administration.

Stopping your business generating new customers is not enough to create this effect. Your rival will have to attack your existing customer base. Through careful research, targeting and relentless attacks, they can take enough existing customers to destabilize your enterprise. Remember, if they target all their competitors at once, their efforts won't be focused enough to have any impact. But if they execute a focused and fast attack against you, and sustain it long enough, you will suffer damage.

If they are successful, they will immediately arrange interviews with all your key employees and gather valuable intelligence on your operations, customers, pricing strategy, supply chains etc. That intelligence will give them everything they need to take your remaining customers and best employees.

You may avoid bankruptcy by raising debt capital. However, this will significantly weaken your business and leave you vulnerable to future attacks. Eventually, through persistence, they will be able to force you into administration.

Attack Targets

- Brand Credibility and Honesty
- Buyers of Products and Services
- Channels of Distribution
- Employees

Attack Methods

- Corporate Espionage
- Employee Poaching
- Falsifying Information
- Murder
- Private Investigators
- Tampering
- Violence

Supply Chains and Channels of Distribution

Overview

Supply chains are critical to a lot of today's business models and competitive advantages. However, in this context, supply chains are not limited to products and covers equipment used in daily operations.

Disrupting your supply chain can slow down the delivery of goods or much needed materials and equipment. The cost of supply can be pushed up so much that it reduces your profit margins, makes your goods so expensive prices must be increased or eliminates your products and services from the market entirely.

The impact of disrupting your supply chains allows your rival to compete with better pricing, quality and delivery efficiency. If their attack is sustained, your business will be at risk from elimination from a given market or region or suffer sufficient damage to give them greater market share.

Similarly, attacking your channels of distribution will stop you shipping goods and services, and collecting revenues.

Attack Targets

- Supplier/Distributor Brands
- Supplier/Distributor Depots
- Supplier/Distributor Employees
- Supplier/Distributor Operations

Attack Methods

- Arson
- Corporate Espionage
- Crime Agency Tips Offs
- Falsifying Information
- Murder
- Poison
- Private Investigators
- Theft
- Violence

ATTACK METHODS

Arson

Arson can be used to attack your infrastructure and communications in a physical way, where other non-physical approaches fail to cause the desired level of devastation, or in combination with non-physical attacks (such as Cyber Crime) to maximize impact. For example, the electrical sub-station that feeds your building with power could be destroyed by fire. Similarly, phone exchanges or internet service boxes can be attacked in a like manner.

However, the most obvious way in which arson will be used is to destroy your physical buildings. It is unlikely yours or your employee's personal addresses will be fire-bombed, unless part of a campaign of violence and intimidation.

Other approaches may include arson attacks against your suppliers and distributors premises, operations and infrastructure.

Case Example

USA, 2011 – On October 20th, Florida duo Sean Everett Davidson, 23, and Bryan David Sullivan, 22, were arrested in connection to an arson attack that reduced a Papa John's Pizza establishment to ashes. The two men worked for rival firm Dominos.

While there were no injuries from the fire, the Lake City Papa John's in northern Florida was 'gutted' according to officials.

Police also said Davidson confessed to starting the fire while under interrogation. After questioning Sullivan, who worked at another Dominos outlet, they arrested him as well.

A local paper reported Sullivan as saying his Dominos location would get more business if the Papa John's 'was put out of business'.

The actions of these two individuals was not believed to be sanctioned by anyone else at Dominos.

Source: https://www.dailymail.co.uk/news/article-2055321/Dominos-workers-burn-rival-Papa-Johns-Pizza-try-customers.html

Corporate Espionage

Corporate spies are existing members of your leadership team or other employees who have had incriminating intelligence used as leverage against them, exploiting and force them to perform illegal acts against your organization on behalf of a hostile rival. Similarly, new employees may be acting as undercover agents, or corporate spies may be installed across your supply chains and distribution networks.

Using corporate spies enables hostile rivals to achieve objectives such as obtaining pricing information, trade secrets, customer lists, deals you are working on and more. They are also used to perform a range of other actions, such as bugging offices and meeting rooms, or performing acts of sabotage, such as delivering viruses into your IT network, compromising communications, performing acts of physical destruction and so on.

Corporate spies are also used to uncover and leak sensitive information to support legal actions against your organization, or undermine your ability to raise capital and attract investors. These could include intelligence on activity that strengthens criminal investigations or civil litigation, or destroy confidence in your organizations longevity or highlight your riskiness as an investment. For example, this information could point to financial trouble as a result of your leadership, financial impropriety, poor financial management, failed financial investments, falling sales statistics, spiraling costs, consistent failure to land big deals, a pattern of losing deals to rivals etc. It may also include intelligence on covered up criminal activity, negligence and liability, which may have been caused or instigated by the corporate spy. If your organization is leaking information, you have a corporate spy.

Another use for corporate spies is to have them create and/or playout scenarios that lead to claims against your insurance policies, or invalidate them altogether. For example, they may cause accidents or injuries to themselves, other employees or members of the public. By using an internal agent, spurious claims can become substantiated and enable your rival (or independent individuals) to bring actions against you. Similarly, they may become a whistle blower for activity they have instigated. These actions may not be covered by your policies and result in you failing to get insurance in the future.

Corporate spies can also be used to attack the brands of your suppliers and distributors, where the attack does not appear to be targeted at you, but damages your routes to market. Similarly, the operations of your suppliers and distributors may also be targeted by Private Investigators, who may be able to uncover sensitive or incriminating evidence that is subsequently used to bribe or blackmail the business owner to increase their prices to your organization, or supply your rival instead of you.

One very subtle, but highly effective, use of corporate spies is to leak information about deals your business is working on and the prices you're pitching at. Your hostile rival can use that information to offer a more commercially attractive package to your prospects and existing customers, stopping you from winning new business and retaining accounts.

Case Example

USA, 2009 – In April 2009, Starwood accused Hilton of a "massive" case of corporate espionage. After being acquired by private equity group Blackstone, Hilton employed 10 managers and senior executives from Starwood.

Starwood accused Hilton of stealing corporate information relating to its luxury brand concepts, claiming they had been used in setting up Hilton's Denizen hotels. Former head of its luxury brands group, Ron Klein, was accused of downloading "truckloads of documents" from a corporate laptop to his own personal email account.

Source: https://en.m.wikipedia.org/wiki/Industrial_espionage

Corporate Sabotage

Corporate sabotage is acts of vandalism or theft that are carried out by corporate spies, such as compromised employees or hired specialists. It is very easy for someone who already has access to your buildings and infrastructure to undertake such attacks. However, if the perpetrator does not have access, specialist skill sets are likely to be employed.

For example, you may have data deleted from systems, purposeful flood damage to server rooms, stolen data from CRM systems, destruction of IT equipment, uploading of viruses and malware, planting of listening or recording devices, physical destruction or theft of company property, corruption of software source code – the list is endless.

In extreme circumstances, you, as a business leader, could be targeted to remove you from your position. An attack of this nature is designed to destabilize your organization, topple share prices or install a specific individual in exchange for favorable deals or competitive alliances.

Case Example

Equatorial Guinea, 2004 – An extreme case of corporate sabotage took place in Equatorial Guinea in the form of a failed coup d'état, known as the Wonga Group. While this might appear to be a military action, which it was, those behind the attempt were British financiers trying to install their own government in exchange for preferential oil rights.

The incident immediately became an international sensation after evidence that the former British Prime Minister, Margret Thatcher's son, Sir Mark Thatcher, was involved in funding the coup. He was subsequently convicted and fined in South Africa. Originally, Thatcher was arrested at his home in Constantia, Cape Town, South Africa, in August 2004. Charges against him related to funding and logistical assistance for the attempted coup, organized by Thatcher's friend and former SAS soldier, Simon Mann.

During his trial in 2008, Simon Mann said that Thatcher "was not just an investor, he came completely on board and became a part of the management team" of the coup plot.

Source: https://en.wikipedia.org/wiki/2004_Equatorial_Guinea_coup_d

%27%C3%A9tat_attempt#:~:text=The%202004%20Equatorial%20Guinea%20coup,could%20carry%20out%20the%20plot.

Crime Agency Tip Offs

Tipping off crime agencies (Customs, Police, Financial Conduct Authorities and Trade Bodies etc.) is exactly what it sounds like. Whether the claims are false or not is irrelevant, providing information to the police or similar investigative agencies is quick, easy and cheap, with potentially catastrophic complications for your business. For example, your rival may inform Customs and/or Drug Enforcement Agencies that your shipments are being used to smuggle drugs and/or weapons in or out of the country. They may also inform the Police of criminal activities, such money laundering or the use of slave labor in foreign or domestic workforces. You may also be targeted individually with accusations of sexual abuse, drug use, soliciting prostitutes or other criminal activity.

By bringing crime agencies into your commercial dealings, possibly into your personal life or the lives of your employees, your rival is seeking to cause reputational damage to your brand and disruption to your business operations. This will have a direct impact on your cash flow and business growth, and will cost you a lot of downtime and money fighting legal proceedings.

In most cases, if you've nothing to hide, you will get through it, but at a cost. However, once the police believe there is something to find, they usually find something. This is why anonymous tips offs are seen as worthy of the effort.

Case Example

South Africa, 2016 – British American Tobacco is accused of corporate espionage against rival cigarette makers in South Africa.

According to court documents, two former police officers working for private investigators paid cash to South African police officials to disrupt British American Tobacco's competitors' business operations.

Court affidavits say British American Tobacco officials instructed the two men to disrupt rivals' trade by falsely suggesting they were marketing and selling cigarettes unlawfully. The aim, often successful, was to get rivals' stock impounded and discourage wholesalers from dealing with rival firms.

These claims against British American Tobacco come after bribery allegations, revealed by the BBC, were passed to the UK's Serious Fraud Office by Paul Hopkins, a British American Tobacco whistleblower who worked for their South African operations.

In a dossier passed to British officials, Mr. Hopkins said he facilitated payments on British American Tobacco's account to destroy anti-smoking laws in several East African countries. He also claimed payments were also made to officials to undermine efforts by the World Health Organization to reduce deaths from smoking, that he ran a corporate spying operation and conducted "black ops" to put rivals out of business. After his claims, members of the US Congress called for a Department of Justice investigation.

British American Tobacco insists the company does not "tolerate corruption in our business anywhere in the world" and says its policy "is to take all appropriate action" on any allegation.

Source: https://www.independent.co.uk/news/world/africa/british-american-tobacco-accused-corporate-espionage-south-africa-a6900731.html

Criminal Damage

Criminal damage is much like corporate sabotage, only it is carried out by personnel who do not have access to your buildings and may have closer ties with the hostile rival. While many of the methods covered in the arson section would count as criminal damage, this section focuses more on other forms of destruction and disruption.

For example, arson can be used to burn down electric sub-stations, phone exchanges and internet service boxes, whereas criminal damage focuses on cutting electric, phone and internet service cables.

Other methods can be applied too, such as blocking or puncturing sanitation systems to shut down factories, offices, retail spaces and hospitality venues. Or, slashing fleet vehicle tires or cutting brake or fuel lines. In very rare situations, you may be the victim of an electromagnetic pulse, which will destroy your electronic communications devices and those of your neighboring businesses.

Case Example

UK, 2019 – A former estate agent was jailed after seeking revenge on a competitor who complained about his advertising practices.

Martin Hobbs, 44, broke into a block of flats and a restaurant, which were owned by the husband of his competitor, and caused over £33,000 of criminal damage.

CCTV footage showed the defendant entering the building through a small window. He tried to obscure security cameras with latex gloves, but he was clearly visible and recognizable.

As a result of the damaged caused by Hobbs, the restaurant could not be opened on schedule and staff who had been hired had to be let go.

The court heard that the offence had been committed against a background of bad feeling between Hobbs and the building owner's wife, a rival estate agent.

Hobbs was jailed for 12 months and served a further 12 months on license upon his release.

Source: https://propertyindustryeye.com/ex-estate-agent-jailed-after-revenge-attack-on-rival-caused-over-33000-of-damage/

Cyber-Crime

As our reliance on technology has increased, so too has cyber-crime which is now prevalent across the globe. Most businesses are familiar with it in some capacity. For instance, your IT systems will undoubtedly be protected from viruses and similar threats. However, when a rival is hostile, cyber-crime can be used in much more creative ways.

Cyber-crime is not always an external attack trying to penetrate your defensive systems. With the use of corporate spies, attacks can be launched from within. Viruses, Trojans and Worms are familiar, but Malware and Spyware less so.

Phishing attacks are also on the rise globally. Most of us can identify them with ease, but more sophisticated attacks are successful, especially if the hostile rival has a corporate spy within your enterprise.

Similarly, organizations are being increasingly hit with DDoS attacks from external sources. With the right technology in place, this shouldn't be a problem. But, when combined with an internal covert action carried out by a corporate spy, a DDoS attack can carve its way through your technological infrastructure in seconds. The results can be catastrophic.

Cyber-crime may also be used to attack your apps, creating actual or perceived vulnerabilities that result in customers ceasing their use of them, or lead to rumors of personal data being leaked or sold to foreign organizations or criminal gangs. Your email servers may also be targeted to take them down, hack into them or blacklist them.

Case Example

China, 2006 – In a report by cyber-security company McAfee, they highlighted one of the world's largest and coordinated cyberattacks involving more than 70 companies, governments, and non-profit organizations that were hacked by spies starting in 2006. McAfee did not name the perpetrator in its report.

Dell SecureWorks, another security company, traced the same attacks to a source in China. Victims of these attacks included a U.S. real estate company, a New York media organization, defense contractors, a South Korean steel and construction firm, the International Olympic Committee, and the World Anti-Doping Agency.

Hackers took information from some of the victims over a period as long as two years.

While the perpetrators of these attacks are unknown, it is likely hostile rivals performed these actions for financial and/or political gain.

Source: https://www.bloomberg.com/news/photo-essays/2011-09-20/famous-cases-of-corporate-espionage

Employee Poaching

Employee poaching is something we've all done or had done to us. However, a coordinated attack on your organization can take away your best sales and account management personnel, and sensitive data, insight, and pricing intelligence with them.

By taking all or a significant quantity of these employees from your business, your rival can quickly offer better deals to your customers and steal them too. This will not only bolster their revenue; it will damage your cash flow to such an extent you may not recover.

If your rival is planning an attack of this nature, it will be difficult to identify and stop, especially if your employees collaborate with their timeframes. Before letters of resignation are exchanged, they will have copied and stored all the information they need to hit their sales targets in their new roles. Short of following up with legal action, there is nothing you can do.

Case Example

USA, 1993 – General Motors (GM) accused Volkswagen (VW) of industrial espionage after Jose Ignacio Lopez, GM's chief of production for its Opel division, left to join the German rival with seven other executives.

GM claimed its corporate secrets were used at VW, following the acquisition of its talented executives. After a period of legal negotiations, the two companies agreed to one of the largest out of court settlements of its kind. GM agreed to drop its lawsuits in exchange for VW buying $1 billion of GM parts over a seven year period. In addition, VW agreed to pay GM $100 million.

Source: https://www.bloomberg.com/news/photo-essays/2011-09-20/famous-cases-of-corporate-espionage

Entrapment

Entrapment is a technique used to attack your leadership team and other employees, as a means of obtaining incriminating intelligence that can be used to exploit and force them to perform illegal acts against your organization on behalf of a hostile rival. It is mostly used when Private Investigators fail to uncover sufficient incriminating evidence from other sources.

Often entrapment is employed using bribes, prostitutes, and alcohol and/or drugs, where the target is placed and 'discovered' in a situation that may compromise their continued employment, professional reputation, personal life or liberty. They will then be offered an 'opportunity' to save themselves, which is to act on behalf of the hostile rival. In extreme cases, fictitious evidence of pedophilia, rape and murder are used.

Case Example

India, 2020 – At least 50 Indian business executives and CEOs were caught up in a 'honey trap' operation involving gay dating app, Grindr.

In most cases, after meeting with their hoax 'dates', the victims were ambushed, beaten, robbed, and photographed in the nude, with the perpetrators keeping the photos in hopes of extorting additional valuables.

It is believed the perpetrators took around a month to get friendly with their victims and once they gained their confidence, assured them that their identities were safe. They then set up meetings from which the blackmail was triggered.

The force behind the attacks has yet to be identified.

Source: https://www.rt.com/news/480718-india-executives-blackmail-grindr/

Falsifying Information

We've all heard of fake news, which dominates the modern era of social and mainstream media. Falsifying information can be used against your organization in a wide range of applications, from destroying your brand to disrupting your supply chains to undermining your ability to raise capital. Your attacker will do this anonymously, possibly from foreign territories, with the purpose of changing market perceptions, destroying your brand reputation, triggering legal action, supporting crime agency investigations and so much more.

Short term attacks can have long lasting impacts, from disrupting cash flow to damaging business growth and even edging your enterprise towards bankruptcy.

Examples of attacks include spreading rumors that your apps or websites are vulnerable to attack and likely to result in customer data being sold to a foreign government, organization or criminal gangs who will empty user bank accounts or steal their identities. Email domains may be masked and used to spread miscommunication to your customers or the wider public. Fake online employee accounts may be created and used to post malicious, sexual or racist content that is aligned to your brand. Mirrored corporate social media accounts can be created to look like yours, populated with fake followers so they have a similar or higher volume than your official accounts, and then used to distribute offensive and/or false information. Using hackers, your website may be changed to distribute false information, advertise offers you cannot honor, distribute pornographic images and videos, and publish content that supports other attacks such as litigation claims against your organization. Creating viral content about people having bad experiences or suffering harm from your products and services. Fake news about criminal activity from your organization and/or its employees. Memes that mock your brand, your leadership, your employees or the buyers of your products and services. Memes that mock the claimed benefits and/or safety of your products and services. The possibilities are limitless.

Typically, you can expect to be hit by the following:

- Fake corporate social accounts – designed to hijack social communications from your organization.
- Fake customer communications – designed to directly deliver misinformation to your customers or attack customers with phishing campaigns etc.
- Fake customer reviews – to create a false perception of your business and your offering.
- Fake employee social accounts – created so they can be used to attack your business and your customers in public social forums.
- Fake news – designed to create viral stories with adverse effects on your organization or supply chains and routes to market, or give credibility to reports of criminal activity or financial impropriety within your business.
- Fake social follower generation – designed to encourage social

media platforms to remove or block your legitimate corporate accounts.
- Fake stock market rumors – designed to undermine your ability to raise capital and create a perception of your business as an investment risk.
- Accusatory memes – that suggest negligence or criminal activity by your company.
- Mockery memes – that target and humiliate customer audiences or market segments who are loyal to your brand.
- Toxic link building – designed to increase poor quality backlinks into your website and damage your search engine performance.

Case Example

China, 2015 – KFC sued three Chinese companies for spreading false rumors about them on social media. According to the Associated Press, the three companies spread fake news that included stories such as how KFC uses genetically modified chickens that have "six wings and eight legs."

KFC has demanded 1.5 million yuan ($242,000) in damages, as well as a formal written apology from each company involved.

The case was launched at a time when Chinese authorities relaunched a campaign "to clean up what they call online rumors, negativity, and unruliness." The campaign seeks to put an end to internet marketers that manipulate "online sentiment on behalf of clients by posting false information about competitors."

Source: https://www.eater.com/2015/6/1/8700465/kfc-china-lawsuit-genetically-modified-chickens-eight-legs

Kidnap

Kidnap is not something to be too worried about, as it is unlikely to happen. If a hostile rival is going down the route of violence, kidnap adds unnecessary complications and risks to their operations.

However, kidnap may be used to stop individuals from performing certain duties or responsibilities at specific times. For example, delivering a keynote speech at a high-profile event, or attending a critical business meeting, or pitching to a new client etc. In these circumstances, desperate rivals may drug and kidnap their targets as a means of temporarily removing them from proceedings or posing a risk to their own interests.

Case Example

USA, 2018 – Mark Krivoi is sentenced for kidnapping, kidnapping conspiracy, extortion and extortion conspiracy in connection with the violent assault of a teenage victim who had started a rival cleaning business.

The evidence presented at trial showed that Krivoi and co-defendant Reizin, who are cousins, participated in a violent extortion conspiracy targeting the 19-year-old victim after he had left Reizin's employ to start his own power-washing business. Krivoi and Reizin drove the victim to a secluded location in Sheepshead Bay, held the victim at knifepoint and warned him that Krivoi was a "soldier" in "Bratva," a local motorcycle club whose name means "brotherhood" in Russian. They demanded $10,000 from the victim and when the victim replied that he could not afford to pay that amount, Reizin turned to Krivoi and uttered a Russian word that means "go". Krivoi then repeatedly punched the victim knocking him to the ground, then threatened to kill the victim and bury him on the spot. The victim agreed to pay $5,000, but then contacted the FBI.

Source: https://www.justice.gov/usao-edny/pr/brooklyn-man-convicted-kidnapping-and-extortion-conspiracy

Legal Action

Legal action may be brought against your organization either directly or indirectly from a hostile rival. Where sufficient evidence exists, the rival may bring this action themselves. However, sufficient evidence may exist that has been obtained or 'created' through spurious means. In this scenario the rival will keep their brand out of the picture.

Your organization may be sued in a variety of different ways. For example, your products may have been tampered with and caused injury to a customer who is subsequently encouraged to take legal action or join a class action, or a customer may have been bribed to falsify injury resulting from the use of your products and follow similar legal steps. This is also not limited to customers, as your employees, especially former ones, may also be encouraged to bring legal action against you. For example, existing employees may be coerced into 'gathering or creating' a basis for legal action, then funded by your rival to bring that action against you.

Alternatively, corporate spies can be used to undertake internal operations to create scenarios that cause harm to people or expose gaps in your insurance cover. They may even act as a whistle blower to activities they instigated. This will enable legal action to be brought against you as a means of compromising your insurance cover. These actions may be brought by employees (former or current) or members of the public, who may or may not be aware of the activities of your hostile rival.

If you are attacked in this way you'll be paying a small fortune in legal fees and settlements, and may require crisis management experts to handle the media fallout.

Case Example

UK, 2019 – In a High Court case in the UK, Sports Direct owner, Mike Ashley, was accused of trying to "eliminate a competitor" and "pick up its assets on the cheap" by funding a legal challenge to the deal that rescued Debenhams from administration.

Debenhams was granted a lifeline by landlords through a company voluntary arrangement (CVA) in May, at the expense of 50 planned store closures and 1,200 job losses.

The CVA will see some landlords' rents cut by between 35 and 50 per cent, and is being challenged by Combined Property Group (CPC), which owns six properties housing Debenhams stores in England.

Mr. Ashley had been the company's largest shareholder and launched several bids to take control of the retailer. But lenders took control of the company in April after it rejected Mr. Ashley's offer of £200m, in part because of his desire to take over as chief executive.

Now, after dropping a legal challenge of its own against Debenhams in July, Sports Direct is funding CPC's lawsuit to overturn the CVA that took the company out of administration.

At a hearing in London, Debenhams' barrister, Tom Smith QC, said that

Sports Direct seemed to want to "drive Debenhams into administration so that it can pick up its assets on the cheap", adding that such an objective "would be consistent with Sports Direct's recent modus operandi".

Source: https://www.independent.co.uk/news/business/mike-ashley-debenhams-legal-challenge-cva-sports-direct-administration-a9089326.html

Murder

Murder can be done in many different ways, depending on how the hostile rival wants it to appear. For example, some murders may be staged to look like industrial accidents or as if they were committed by a targeted individual. They may also be carried out like an execution to send a message to you or someone else. Others may include car bombs, lethal poisons and so on, designed to throw suspicion away from the perpetrator or be un-traceable/solvable.

In business-to-business war craft, murder is used as an escalation of violence to convert people to corporate spies or force an individual to take an extreme action, or to remove important members of an organization so it becomes unstable. Murder has also been used to avoid making payments, claim on life insurance policies, dispose of corporate spies when they are no longer needed, eliminate and intimidate investors and/or bankers, disrupt supply chains and channels of distribution, or as a means of counterattack against a hostile rival seeking to entrap and exploit employees.

However, murder can also be used to simulate industrial accidents and bring investigations that lead to imprisonment for you and/or members of your leadership team, and/or claims against your business and your insurance policies. Similarly, members of the public may be murdered and staged to look like your products, services or employees were responsible, leading to a collapse in your new sales revenues and loss of current customers.

However, murder doesn't stop there. In some cases, your investors may be targeted directly or through their families in order to stop you raising funds. Depending on how the murder is carried out, this can also send shockwaves through the investment community and intimidate other investors into avoiding you altogether.

Generally, there are six approaches:

- to murder you, a member of your leadership team or a key employee
- to murder a member of your family, or that of a member of your leadership team or employee's families
- to murder a third-party as a method of framing or entrapping you, a member of your leadership team or other employees
- to murder a third-party or you or a member of your leadership team or key employee, making it look like an industrial accident
- to murder an investor or banker, or a member of their family, in order to stop you raising capital or intimidate other investors into avoiding your organization
- to murder an employee of a supplier or distributor, to eliminate that organization or stop them supplying to you

Case Example

UK, 1999 – In 1999, British property magnate, Nicholas van Hoogstraten, hired men to attack one of his business associates, Mohammed Sabir Raja.

On the morning of 2 July 1999, two of Hoogstraten's hired thugs, disguised as handymen, arrived at Raja's residence. When Raja answered the door a fight quickly broke out. Raja was stabbed five times in the heart and neck and was shot in the head twice at point blank range, dying as a consequence.

In July 2002, van Hoogstraten was sentenced to 10 years' imprisonment for the manslaughter of Raja, after being found not guilty of murder. A jury at the trial decided that "although he clearly wanted Mr. Raja harmed, there is no evidence that he had intended Mr. Raja to be murdered".

However, on 19 December 2005, the family of Raja, in a civil action against van Hoogstraten, was awarded £6 million by Mr. Justice Lightman, after the court found that the balance of probabilities was "that the recruitment of the two thugs was for the purpose of murdering Mr. Raja and not merely to frighten, threaten or hurt him".

Source: https://en.m.wikipedia.org/wiki/Nicholas_van_Hoogstraten

Poison

Poison may be used as a method for murder, but in this context it is non-lethal. For example, poison can be used in a similar way to infection, as a means of disrupting business operations or temporarily incapacitating targeted individuals.

As with infection, your rival may poison personnel working within your supply chains or channels of distribution. This is of course designed to slow down your production and delivery of goods and services and impact your cash flow.

However, an individual may be poisoned to stop them performing certain tasks at a specific point in time. For example, you may be at a trade event and giving a presentation the next day. The night before, you may have your drink or food spiked with an agent that renders you too ill to go on stage the next day. Similar approaches have been used to stop people attending important meetings, delivering services, or completing projects.

Human infection differs from poisoning, although the methods of transmission may be similar. When it comes to hostile rivals, they will stop at nothing to win and that can mean purposefully infecting you, your leadership team, your employees, your customers or the workforce of your suppliers and distributors.

By infecting members of your organization, they can reduce your productivity or force targeted establishments to close. They may even render individuals incapable of returning to work, or create a media scandal if multiple HIV or AIDS infections are established. In contrast, infecting your customers can cause legal action against your organization and will certainly create bad publicity, especially if the infection can be proven to have originated from one of your premises.

Your rival may also infect personnel working within your supply chains or channels of distribution. This is of course designed to slow down your production and delivery of goods and services, and impact your cash flow. However, publically known infection outbreaks with your suppliers can also impact market confidence in your products and lead to a drop in sales.

Case Example

China, 2002 – Chen Zhengping confessed to planting poison in the food of his rival in Nanjing. He was quickly put on trial and sentenced to death.

There was panic and anger throughout the city after the news of the mass poisoning spread. Most of the victims were school children and workers buying breakfast snacks before attending classes or going to work. Many quickly fell unconscious and foamed at the month. More than 200 were rushed to eight hospitals.

Chen fled the scene and was caught the next day on a train about 370 miles north of Nanjing. He is said to have confessed promptly, explaining that he was resentful of his rival's success.

Chen used a brand of rat poison that was banned since the mid-1990s.

Source: https://www.theguardian.com/world/2002/oct/01/internationaleducationnews.china

Private Investigators

Private Investigators are commonly used by organizations to acquire sensitive information. However, they can also be used to obtain damning intelligence on individuals and their activities. This makes them easier to manipulate and exploit. It is typically the first action when seeking to acquire corporate spies, compromise routes to market, damage sales performance, undermine your ability to raise capital and more.

Usually the Private Investigator will target people within your organization to uncover irregularities in social and professional relationships, finances, past employment and education history, criminal history and, past and present behavior. They will also identify weaknesses such as alcohol or opiate dependency, gambling habits, extra-marital affairs, use of drugs or prostitutes and illegal business dealings. The list is endless. Outside of your organization, investors, bankers, owners of your supply chain businesses or those of your distributors may all be targeted.

However, Private Investigators may also dig into your business, its financial arrangements, domestic and overseas operations, supply chains and more. This also applies to third party organizations with links to yours. Anything they find, which suggests any impropriety, will be used as ammunition for direct or indirect legal action, crime agency tip offs, undermining investor confidence, disrupting or destroying supply chains and channels of distribution and, destroying your brand. The evidence will be 'leaked' to news networks, media outlets and distributed across social media.

Private investigators can also be employed to find people willing to bring legal action against your organization from injury or loss, and find the evidence to substantiate those claims (whether they are true or not).

Case Example

Switzerland, 2019 – According to reports in Bloomberg, a lawyer representing the security business Investigo says a Credit Suisse contractor, who hired the firm to investigate a former top executive, had committed suicide.

The contractor had hired Investigo investigators to look into Iqbal Khan after the star banker moved to co-head the wealth-management division of rival bank UBS. Credit Suisse worried Khan would persuade other employees to join him.

On September 17, Khan was said to have noticed he was being followed and approached an investigator in his car. Khan confronted the lone investigator and attempted to take photographs of him using a cellphone. The investigator blocked the picture using his hands and went away. But Khan reportedly said that he noticed three men following him and his wife who then attempted to take his phone away from him, leading to a physical altercation.

Swiss media reported that several people suspected of the pursuit were arrested after Khan filed a complaint.

Source: https://fortune.com/2019/10/01/credit-suisse-banker-spying-investigator-dead/

Tampering

Tampering can be achieved using corporate spies from inside your organization, your supply chains, or your channels of distribution. By tampering with your products, hostile rivals can cause them to malfunction or cause harm to customers, damaging your brand reputation and opening legal action against you. However, it also causes your customers to go elsewhere and significantly reduces your new sales revenues, massively slashing your growth and choking your cash flow.

Case Example

USA, 2019 – A rival business owner spat, picked her nose, and urinated into containers at a rival ice cream parlor.

Investigators allege that Jung Soon Wypcha, 66, was caught on videotape engaging in a series of vile acts at Lu Lu's Ice Cream shop in Indian Shores, a town about 20 miles west of St. Petersburg.

Wypcha, who runs the Indian Shores Food Mart, was arrested and charged with tampering with consumer products and criminal mischief, both felonies.

The ice cream shop, which was forced to close for a period of time, since reopened and its owners believe that Wypcha targeted the business due to a fear of competition.

Source: http://www.thesmokinggun.com/documents/revolting/ice-cream-tamper-arrest-639502

Theft

Theft is something we all live with every day, but thankfully we're not all victims of it. However, when a hostile rival wants something you've got, or simply doesn't want you to have, they will try to take it. For example, in the context of infrastructure, a rival may steal devices, vehicles or other important assets simply to stop you using them. However, the majority of cases will involve something they want.

Some rivals may steal your products and push them into the market via criminal gangs, undercutting your market price and taking custom away from your distributors. This is an extremely risky attack. They may even target your suppliers to stop you getting much needed materials and equipment or acquire those supplies for their own production operations, allowing them to produce goods faster and cheaper than you.

However, most theft from your organization is likely to go un-detected. For example, stealing copies of source code (if you are a software company), CRM customer data, pricing information, secret formulas or recipes, future strategic plans and more.

Case Example

Israel, 2009 – Executives from Swissport were taken into questioning in order to determine details of alleged theft. Police suspected the shipping company at Ben-Gurion Airport stole hundreds of thousands of shekels worth of equipment from a competing firm.

Ben-Gurion police infiltrated a facility belonging to cargo firm Swissport and seized equipment that they believe was stolen from competitor Maman.

The equipment in question includes platforms for loading cargo into planes, each one worth around 600 Euros. When police entered the Swissport storehouse, they reportedly found 120 platforms, with several showing signs that someone had tried to remove the MMN logo from them.

Source: https://www.haaretz.com/1.5084860

Violence

Hostile rivals use violence more than you may think and in doing so, order or undertake operations more typically associated with organized crime. Violence is usually applied to situations where your rival needs to intimidate people, remove enemies or remove witnesses to crimes.

In terms of intimidation, violence may often be used against you, your leadership team or your employees, or investors and bankers who are interested in providing capital to your organization, and is typically the first step in an escalation of threats and actions that ends with murder. This is almost always used when initial threats are not taken seriously, or individuals refuse to co-operate with demands to become corporate spies or perform specific actions on behalf of the hostile rival.

Violence is also used to threaten employees into bringing legal action against your organization, whether that is in the civil or criminal courts. It may also be used on members of the public for the same reasons. In some cases, violence can be used against the people listed here to stage injuries that are claimed to have resulted from use of your products and/or services, or following interaction with a member of your organization. This is to create a credible claim against your business and your insurance policies, damage your sales growth and motivate customers to abandon you.

Acts of violence can also be used against your suppliers and distributors.

Just like with murder, there are six approaches:

- to attack you, a member of your leadership team or a key employee
- to attack a member of your family, or that of a member of your leadership team or employee's families
- to attack a third-party as a method of framing or entrapping you, a member of your leadership team or other employees
- to attack a third-party or you or a member of your leadership team or key employee, forcing them to take actions against their will
- to attack an investor or banker, or a member of their family, in order to stop you raising capital or intimidate other investors into avoiding your organization
- to attack an employee of a supplier or distributor, to stop them supplying to you

Case Example

UK, 1968 – At 22, British property magnate, Nicholas van Hoogstraten was convicted for paying a gang to throw a grenade into the house of Rabbi Bernard Braunstein. Braunstein's son David owed a debt to van Hoogstraten over a failed textile business they had jointly owned. Van Hoogstraten had become dissatisfied with a repayment arrangement the two men had made.

He was sentenced to a four-years in prison in May 1968, and a further four-years the following August, to run concurrently, after an appeal.

Van Hoogstraten was arrested immediately after his release and was subsequently jailed on eight counts of handling stolen goods. In October

1972, he was sentenced to a further 15 months for bribing prison officers to smuggle him luxuries.

Source: https://en.m.wikipedia.org/wiki/Nicholas_van_Hoogstraten

www.ingramcontent.com/pod-product-compliance
Lightning Source LLC
Chambersburg PA
CBHW070900220526
45466CB00005B/2061